Optical *Illusions*

By L. C. Casterline
and the Editors of
Ripley Entertainment Inc.

Illustrations by Gen Shibuya, Hal Just,
and the Ripley Archives

tangerine
Press®

Photo Credits

Ripley Entertainment Inc. and the editors of this book wish to thank the following photographers, agents, and other individuals for permission to use and reprint the following photographs in this book. Any photographs included in this book that are not acknowledged below are property of the Ripley Archives. Great effort has been made to obtain permission from the owners of all materials included in this book. Any errors that may have been made are unintentional and will gladly be corrected in future printings if notice is sent to Ripley Entertainment Inc., 5728 Major Boulevard, Orlando, Florida 32819.

PP. 4, 24, 27, 57, 66: Gen Shibuya

p. 26: Painter's Easel with a Fruit Piece by Cornelius N. Gysbrechts. 1668/72. Statens Museum for Kunst/Copenhagen/Denmark/Erich Lessing/Art Resource/NY

p. 29: M. C. Escher's "Sky and Water I" © 2002 Cordon Art B.V. - Baarn - Holland. All rights reserved.

p. 37: Geologic "Face on Mars" Formation/NASA; View of "Face on Mars"/NASA/JPL/Malin Space Science Systems

p. 49: Moon Steps—Seattle © Shay Stephens 2001

p. 54: Gateway Arch, St. Louis, MO/PhotoDisc

p. 65: M. C. Escher's "Ascending and Descending" © 2002 Cordon Art B.V. - Baarn - Holland. All rights reserved.

Developed by Nancy Hall, Inc.
Designed by Atif Toor and Gen Shibuya

ISBN 0-439-51204-2
12 11 10 9 8 7 6 5 4 3 2 1   3 4 5 6 7 8 / 0
Lenticular made in the U.S.A. Printed in China.
First printing, December 2002

SEEING IS BELIEVING!

Robert Ripley traveled the world looking for amazing facts, oddities, and curiosities that seemed unbelievable, but were really true. He learned about many more from his fans, who sent him letters and drawings—more than 3,500 a day—hoping he would feature them in a Believe It or Not! cartoon. Ripley was interested in everything: extraordinary people and animals, incredible discoveries and inventions, remarkable natural wonders, and surprising optical illusions.

Why are optical illusions unbelievable? Because if you're like most people, you trust your eyes, you believe what you see. And you may find it hard to believe that something that looks so obvious is not quite what you think it is.

OPTICAL MEANS "OF OR RELATING TO SIGHT." AN ILLUSION IS SOMETHING THAT IS MISLEADING.

HOW
CAN THIS HAPPEN?

It all starts with vision. You may see things with your eyes, but it's your brain that figures out what your eyes are seeing. Look at this picture of a quarter.

It probably looks round to you even though your eyes are seeing an oval. Why? Because your brain knows that quarters are round.

Watch as a friend walks away from you. Is he or she really getting smaller or does it just look that way? While riding in a car, have you ever seen a puddle of water in the road ahead that's gone when you get there? When someone uses a flashbulb to snap your picture, do you see a dark spot for a few seconds afterward? Have you ever been scared by a shadow that looked like a person or an animal? Illusions are everywhere once you start to notice them.

You'll find lots of optical illusions in this book. Sometimes you'll have to lift the book up, move it around, or even turn it upside down to see the full effect of the illusion. Because not everyone sees things the same way, some of the illusions may not fool you. If you "don't get" an illusion, try showing it to a friend. Perhaps he or she will be able to see it. You can even make some of the illusions yourself.

So what are you waiting for? Start reading— and looking. You'll be amazed by the things you see.

Believe It!®

 When you see a numbered symbol like the one on the left, look in the answer key starting on page 76 to find the answers to questions and/or more information about the illusion. The answers to the riddles are on page 80.

A word about the cover: You may be wondering what a man who swallows a mouse has to do with optical illusions. He really did swallow a mouse and bring it back up again unharmed, so that's not an illusion. What is? The way we made the picture on the cover look as if it's moving. We also used another trick to . . . well, why don't you read all about it on pages 74–75? Meanwhile, try flipping the top right-hand corners of the pages to animate your own version of the mouse-swallower.

NOW YOU SEE IT—
NOW YOU DON'T

Seeing is not always believing. You've probably heard of mirages appearing to people in the desert. Well, here's one that fooled explorers in the Arctic . . .

On a polar expedition in 1906, Robert Peary sighted a range of mountain peaks far to the northwest of Greenland. He named his discovery Crocker Land, and it appeared on at least one map. But when Donald Macmillan, another explorer, saw the high peaks seven years later, he learned from an Inuit that it was only a mirage!

Luckily, you don't have to go to the desert or the Arctic to see things that aren't really there. Here are some mirages you can see right in your own room.

1 You don't have a hole in your hand—or do you? Try this and find out. Roll a piece of letter-sized paper into a long tube. Hold the tube up to one eye and look at something about ten feet away. Hold your free hand up next to the tube, about halfway down. What do you see?

THE BORDERS BETWEEN HOT AND COLD AIR MASSES CAN ACT AS A MIRROR, REFLECTING AN IMAGE FROM ONE PLACE TO ANOTHER.

2 Now try this. Face a blank wall a couple of feet away from you. Bring your hands up to eye level and hold them as shown, keeping your index fingers an inch or two apart. Stare at the wall between your fingers. Do you see an extra finger floating there?

3 Facing a window, TV screen, or computer monitor, hold one finger out in front of you. Look at it with one eye closed. Now quickly open that eye and close the other one. What happens?

4 Can you turn the two lines below into three? Hold the book sideways just below eye level, keeping it at a right angle to your eyes. How many lines do you see now?

5 Stare at the center of the figure below while holding the book sideways about two inches away from your face. Do you see more than one figure?

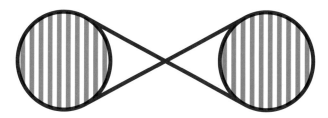

6 Bring the page close to your face, looking steadily at the space between the dog's head and the cat's. Can you make them touch noses?

EACH EYE SEES THINGS FROM A SLIGHTLY DIFFERENT ANGLE. YOUR BRAIN PUTS THE PICTURES TOGETHER TO FORM ONE IMAGE.

THE **WHIRLING CLOUD** of MOUNT JIRINAJ (Indonesia)
A FLAT CLOUD
HOVERING OVER THE PEAK OF AN EXTINCT VOLCANO
AFFECTED BY HOT AIR RISING FROM THE CRATER,
SPINS SWIFTLY AROUND AND AROUND

Hot air makes the cloud of Mount Jirinaj swirl in circles, but the movement you'll see in the following illusions are all in your mind!

7 Gaze at the image on the right while you move the page around in a tight circle. What do you see?

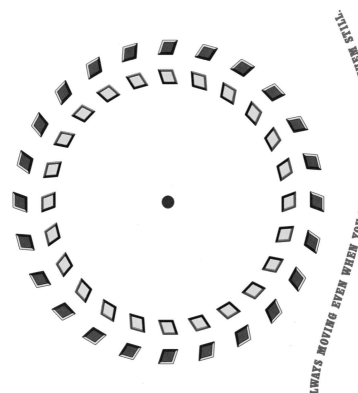

8 Look at the dot in the center of the two circles, then move the page slowly toward you and away. What happens?

You don't even have to move the page to see movement in the next two pictures.

9 Move your eyes around while looking at the grid. What do you see?

10 Can you see the swirls radiating out from the center of this picture? Do you see anything else that isn't really there?

BELIEVE IT OR NOT! A PERSON WITH ONE EYE CAN SEE MORE THAN A PERSON WITH TWO EYES. CAN YOU FIGURE OUT HOW?

COLORIFIC

ONCE **A BLUE MOON** APPEARED IN AUSTRALIA
IT WAS CAUSED BY A TREMENDOUS DUST
STORM CONTAINING MYRIADS OF SPECKS
OF SILICA OXIDE WHICH CUT OUT THE RED
AND YELLOW
RAYS
- LEAVING ONLY THE BLUE

Sometimes things aren't quite what they seem.

When a full moon appears twice in one month, the second one is called a "blue moon."

▶ The diagonal lines below are black and white—or are they? Look carefully. Do you see any colors?

12 Besides black and white sensors (called rods), your eyes have three kinds of color sensors (called cones): red, blue, and green. If you are missing one or more color sensors, you may not be able to see certain colors. In the early 20th century, Shinobu Ishihara developed a test for color blindness. Look at the circles. Can you see numbers in them?

MORE MEN (ABOUT 10%) ARE COLOR BLIND THAN WOMEN (LESS THAN 1%).

NOTE: If you can't see one of the numbers, you may be color blind. Ask your parents to have the eye doctor test you.

Each word below is printed in a different color. Say the names of the printed colors (not the words) out loud. Tricky, huh?

red **green** **blue**

orange **black**

yellow **gray** **purple**

red **pink** **white**

13 Which red diamonds in the figure below are darker?

Keep your eye on the hazy spot in the center of the figure below. What happens to it?

THE STRANGE SNOW FUNNELS OF THE HIMALAYAS

HUGE CRATERS
LINED WITH IRIDESCENT GREEN ICE
HAVE SUCH A HYPNOTIC EFFECT

*THAT TRAVELERS FEEL AN URGE TO
LEAP INTO THE DAZZLING PIT*

ALL THE COLORS YOU SEE ARE A REFLECTION OF LIGHT. WITHOUT LIGHT, YOU WOULD SEE ONLY BLACK.

DRAWING THE SHADES

Red, orange, yellow, green, blue, purple, and violet are the easiest colors to see in a rainbow. They are the main colors of the "visible spectrum," the wavelengths of color that people are able to see. But there are many different shades of these colors.

15 Are the inner circles in the center of the top pair of squares the same color? How about the pair on the bottom?

16 Which set of green lines is darker?

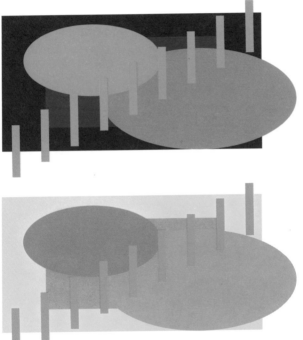

YOUR EYES CAN DETECT UP TO SEVEN MILLION DIFFERENT SHADES OF COLOR.

Look at the pictures in this book with a magnifying glass. Can you see the dots? The book was printed with only four colors: magenta (red), yellow, cyan (blue), and black. Each dot is one of these colors. All the other colors you see depend on which color dots overlap and how close together they are.

SNAPSHOTS

17 Look steadily at each of the following two pictures for 30 seconds or more, then look at a blank piece of white paper. What do you see?

When you've looked at the pictures long enough, then look away, your eyes "remember" them, but in the opposite color. Black becomes white and green becomes red.

18 Now try your own experiments. Stare at a lemon, then at a sheet of white paper. What color does it turn into? How about an orange?

19 Here are some more things to observe. Did the reverse image of the light bulb look brighter than the white of the paper? Instead of looking at the afterimage on paper, try looking at a wall about ten feet away. How does the afterimage look now? After you've stared at the pictures or objects for almost 30 seconds, what do you see appearing around the edges?

THE **STRANGE SHADOW OF THE SIERRA NEVADA**
Venezuela
EVERY MOUNTAIN CLIMBER IN THE EARLY-MORNING HOURS CASTS UPON THE ADJACENT CLOUDS **A SHADOW 100 FEET HIGH**

OPPOSITE COLORS ON THE COLOR WHEEL ARE CALLED "COMPLEMENTARY COLORS."

WHICH WAY IS UP?

TOYAMA BAY IN UOZO, JAPAN, IS THE SITE OF NATURAL MIRAGES EVERY SPRING WHERE THE IMAGES OF SHIPS, BUILDINGS, AND TREES ARE SEEN *FLOATING UPSIDE-DOWN OVER THE WATER!*

This mirage is unusual because everything appears upside down. Try these experiments and see if your eyes can make things switch direction.

20 Hold the page a few inches away from your eyes, tilted slightly down and away from you. Look at the lines from the spot at lower left. Do the lines appear to be standing up from the page?

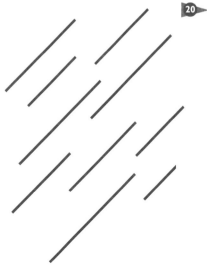

21 Fold a piece of plain white paper in half. Stand it up on the table like a tent. While sitting down, look at it with one eye. After a moment, the paper should switch direction and look like it is standing upright. Slowly, move your head from side to side. Does the paper look like it's moving? Now try the same thing while standing up. How is it different?

22 Are the cowboy and the horse facing toward you or away from you?

LOOK AGAIN

23 ▸ Things are not always what they seem to be. Except for being upside down, this photo looks pretty normal, right? Now turn it the other way around. Yikes!

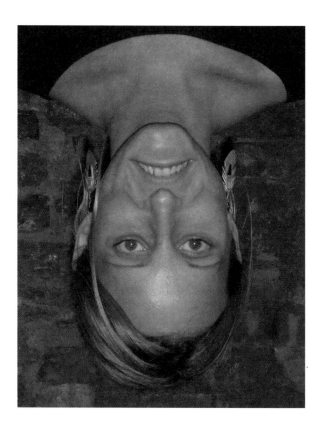

Look closely at this 25-foot-high copy of a self-portrait by Vincent van Gogh. It was created by a Dutch artist named Cornel Bierens from 3,000 postcards—each featuring a painting by Van Gogh.

Tadhiko Okawa used burned toast to create his own version of Mona Lisa, Leonardo da Vinci's famous painting.

The picture below may look like a photograph of a painting on an easel, but it's really an oil painting created by Cornelius N. Gysbrechts in the 1600s.

Artist Richard Haas painted the side of this building at 112 Prince Street in New York City. Years of bright sunlight have faded the painting so the two real windows now stand out from the painted ones.

THIS STYLE OF ULTRA-REALISTIC PAINTING IS CALLED "TROMPE L'OEIL" (PRONOUNCED "TROMP LOY"), WHICH IS FRENCH FOR "TRICK THE EYE."

24 Do you see a vase or something else in this picture?

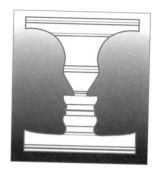

25 Hidden in this flower design are the profiles of a man and a woman. Can you find them?

In Sky and Water I, by M. C. Escher, there are birds at the top and fish at the bottom. But look closely at the middle and you'll see both birds *and* fish.

26 Have you ever seen art that's colorful and has different shapes but doesn't look like a real object or scene? That's called "abstract" art. Is the pattern below really abstract or can you find a five-pointed star hidden within?

TWO FOR ONE

Some things are more than they appear to be!

27 Can you see both a rabbit and a duck?

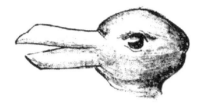

28 A cartoonist named W. E. Hill drew the picture below in 1915. Do you see a young woman or an old woman?

29 The Canadian flag features a maple leaf in the center. But look closely and you may see two men arguing.

This is what you call a real duck pond! It was built inside a bird sanctuary in Manitoba, Canada.

Robert R. Taylor took this aerial photo just as the sun lit up the surface of the pond.

30 Here's something you can try. Draw four arrowheads like the one on the right so that it looks as though you've really drawn five.

NATURAL MIMICS

Nature is filled with animals, plants, and rocks that look like something other than what they are. Here are a few of them.

NATURE'S FLOWER CHILDREN

EACH PINK FLOWER OF THE PURPLE ORCHID LOOKS REMARKABLY LIKE *A SMALL CHILD WEARING A HAT TOO LARGE FOR IT*

TREE TRUNK
WHICH FORMED THE LIKENESS OF *A HUMAN MASK* Lake Garda, Italy

A NATURAL TEMPLE
COMPRISING WHITE CORAL
LIMESTONE COLUMNS AND
A GRANITE ROOF
*CARVED BY THE WATERS
OF THE WEB RIVER,
IN ETHIOPIA*

Travis Robinson of Texarkana, Texas, caught a turtle that had markings like a face on its underside.

THE **PHANTOM SHIP**
A NATURAL ROCK FORMATION
in Crater Lake, Oregon, THAT APPEARS TO BE A
FULL-RIGGED SHIP AND ITS CREW. AN OPTICAL ILLUSION, IT
VANISHES FROM TIME TO TIME BY BLENDING WITH THE CLIFF
BEHIND IT, THEN SUDDENLY REAPPEARS

SEEING THINGS

When you look at these illusions, you may see things that aren't really there.

31 Do you see a triangle?

32 A square?

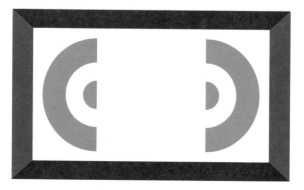

33 Look at the color shapes below. Can you see a word? What is it? Are the letters really there?

34 Are there pale circles between the squares? What happens when you try to look directly at them?

Both Mother Nature and human nature can play tricks on the eyes.

► For several days before the great storm of 1829, two suns were seen in the sky above the Scottish Countryside near the river Spey.

► In 1647, a ship loaded with colonists left New Haven, Connecticut, on its way to England and vanished—until one year later, when it appeared in the sky with amazing vividness.

In 1976, Viking 1 transmitted images of what looked like a face on Mars (below). Some people thought it had been carved by beings who once lived on the planet. In 2001, better images taken by the Mars Global Surveyor's Orbital Camera showed that the "face" was really a natural rock formation (above right).

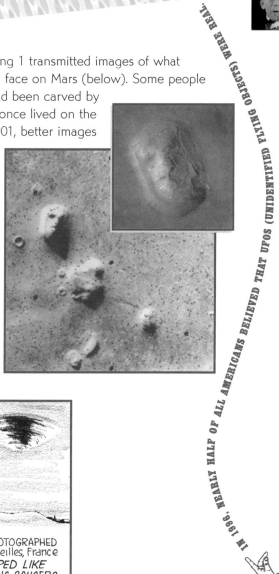

²CLOUDS PHOTOGRAPHED over Marseilles, France
BOTH SHAPED LIKE INVERTED FLYING SAUCERS
Nov. 4, 1954

GETTING IN SHAPE

Your brain can't always tell exactly what your eyes are seeing. Don't believe it? Try looking at the pictures on the next few pages.

35 Is this a spiral or concentric circles? Cover half the picture with your hand. What do you think now?

36 What shape do you see inside the radiating lines?

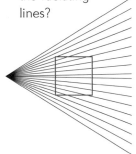

37 Are the red circles below distorted?

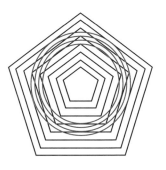

38 Are the inside squares distorted?

39 Which figure is a rectangle and which is a square?

40 Look at the tiles below. Do they look uneven? Test them with a ruler.

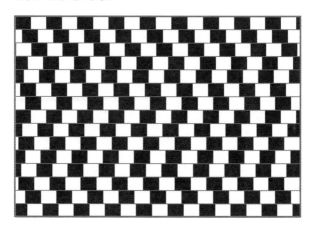

41 Do the purple lines look bent or straight?

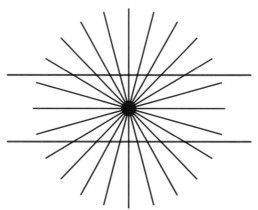

42 How many curved lines did Joe Ganci of Bronx, New York, use to draw this picture?

43 Do these lines look parallel to you?

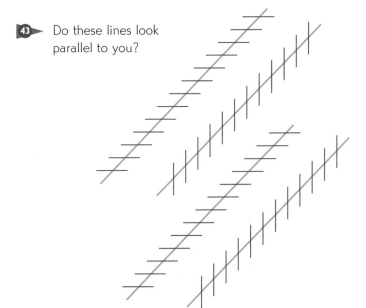

44 Are the red bars in the figure below straight?

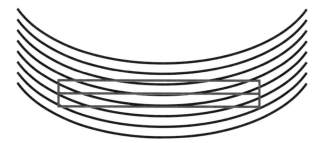

45 Is the center line in the figure on the left straight or slanted?

46 When you look at this checkerboard, you can see that the checks are curved. But hold the page about an inch from your eyes. How do they look now?

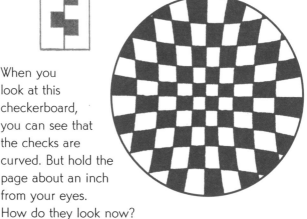

The walls and columns of the Lincoln Memorial in Washington, D.C., appear to be straight, but they actually tilt inward to keep the building from looking as though it bulges out at the top.

47 Do the orange lines below look like they curve?

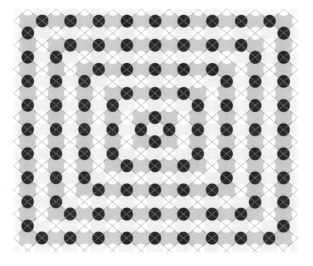

SIZE-WISE

48 Which circle is bigger?

49 Which is larger? The area of the outer ring or the inner circle?

50 Look at the three arcs below. Which one is cut from the largest circle?

51 Try this magic trick. Trace the drawings below on a piece of paper, then cut them out and place them side by side. Which one looks bigger? Now switch places. Which one looks bigger now?

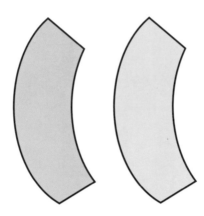

Rainbows are formed when sunlight hits raindrops, which "bend" the light. From the ground, you can only see the rainbow as an arc. But if you're in an airplane and sunlight is shining on rainfall below you, the rainbow will appear as a circle.

RAINBOWS VIEWED from AIRPLANES APPEAR AS COMPLETE CIRCLES!

52 Which inner square is larger?

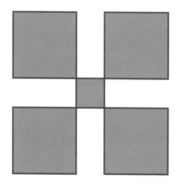

53 The three color bands in the French flag below may look the same, but they're not. The blue section is the smallest; the white section is three percent larger and the red section is seven percent larger. Can you figure out why?

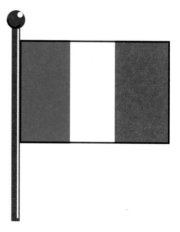

54 Look at the columns in the buildings below. Which ones look thicker? More than 2,000 years ago, the builders of the Parthenon in Greece made the outside columns thicker than the inside ones. Can you figure out why?

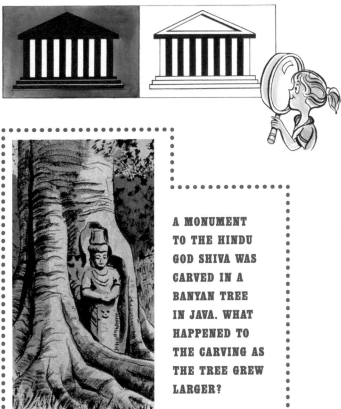

A MONUMENT TO THE HINDU GOD SHIVA WAS CARVED IN A BANYAN TREE IN JAVA. WHAT HAPPENED TO THE CARVING AS THE TREE GREW LARGER?

55 Which red bar is bigger?

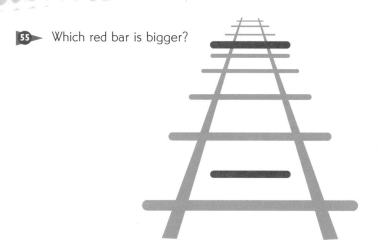

The car in the photo below looks like a 1907 Rolls Royce Silver Ghost—but it isn't. Reg Pollard used more than a million matchsticks to build this life-sized scale model.

▶ Does the full moon look bigger to you when it's near the horizon? If it does, don't worry. It's been fooling people for thousands of years. Time-lapse photographs like this one taken by Shay Stephens of Seattle, Washington, show that the moon is the exact same size whether it's just rising or high in the sky.

▶ In the photo above, you can see the moon change from orange to yellow as it rises higher in the sky. The moon looks orange when it's first rising above the horizon because its light has to travel a greater distance through Earth's atmosphere.

A DIFFERENT PERSPECTIVE

We see the world in three dimensions—height, width, and depth (or distance). A drawing or painting only has two dimensions, so to make a realistic picture, we use "perspective" to give the illusion of depth. To get an idea of how perspective is used in art, look at a long, straight stretch of road or railroad track, or a line of telephone poles. See how they get smaller and smaller? The point where they disappear is called the "vanishing point."

56 Does this picture look flat to you? Or does it look like a wall and a floor?

57 Is one running boy bigger than the other?

ANOTHER KIND OF PERSPECTIVE IS "ATMOSPHERIC" PERSPECTIVE, WHERE ARTISTS USE STRONGER COLORS FOR CLOSE-UP OBJECTS THAN FOR BACKGROUND OBJECTS.

LINING UP

58 Can you tell which line is longer in each set of drawings?

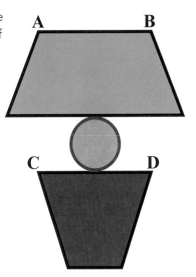

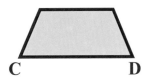

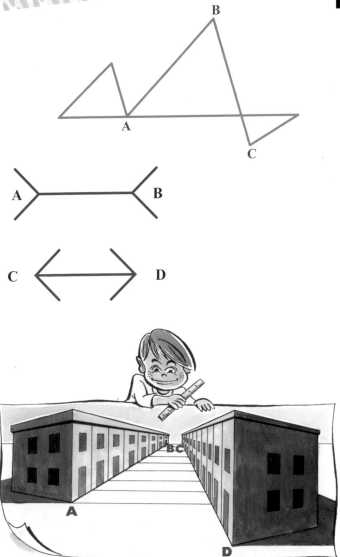

KEEPING YOUR DISTANCE

59 Is the top hat higher than it is wide at the brim?

60 The Gateway Arch in St. Louis, Missouri, is 630 feet tall. Can you figure out how wide it is at the base?

61 Which two eyes are closer together?

62 Is the dot in the pyramid closer to the top or to the bottom?

WILL THE NAIL MOVE HIGHER AS THE TREE GROWS TALLER?

MAKING CONNECTIONS

63 If the green lines were connected, would they form one line?

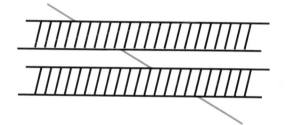

64 Which green line on the left matches up with the green line on the right?

65 Would the two arcs meet to form a circle if you connected them?

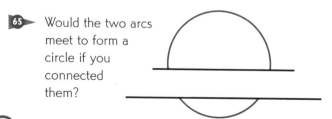

66 Did the artist make a mistake in drawing these arches?

67 Here's an easy trick to try yourself. Fill a glass with water and put in a pencil. Does it look broken like the straw does in the photograph? Try putting your finger in the water. How does it look? This happens because water, which is thicker than air, "bends" light.

DISAPPEARING ACTS

68 Place a postage stamp (or a small piece of colored paper) under a glass of water. Can you still see it? Now put a piece of cardboard or paper about the size of a postcard over the top of the glass. What happens?

69 Each eye is connected to your brain by an optic nerve. Where the nerve leaves your eye, you have a blind spot. Here's how to find it. Hold the book about a foot away, then close your right eye and stare at the boy's face above right. Slowly move the page back and forth. When the girl disappears, you've found the blind spot in your left eye. To find the blind spot in your right eye, close your left eye, stare at the girl's face, and move the page until the boy disappears. Can you figure out why the blind spot doesn't show up when you're just looking around?

DIFFERENT WAYS OF SEEING THINGS

70 Which end of the box is in front? Does it face up or down?

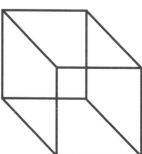

71 Is the ladybug on the inside of the box or the outside?

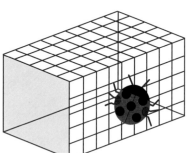

72 Are you looking at the basket from above or beneath?

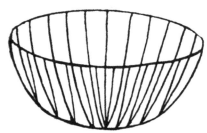

73 Can you see both of the cubes in this picture at the same time?

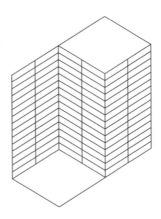

74 Do you see a pyramid or a well?

75 Do you see a sturdy bench or a bench with one leg missing?

76 Do you see a bunch of circles or a tube?

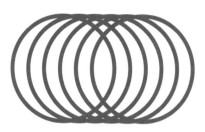

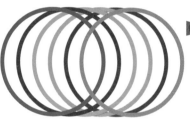

77 How about now? Do the colors make a difference?

78 Does the stairway go up or down?

79 Does this figure curve toward you or away from you?

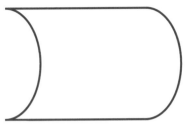

80 Not counting the diamond, what shape do you first notice in the figure below? Can you see another shape?

81 How many prongs do you see in this picture?

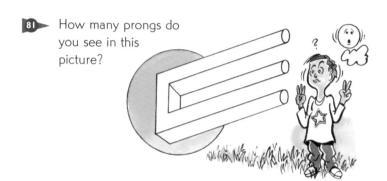

82 Do you think the triangle on the left could be built out of wood?

83 Joseph Shagena of Sebring, Florida, drilled two holes in this bottle, then inserted a wooden arrow. But both ends of the arrow are bigger than the holes he drilled. How did he get the arrow to go through the bottle?

84► How long would it take you to get to the bottom of a stairway like the one pictured in Ascending and Descending, by M. C. Escher?

► This may look like the body of a merman, but it's really the front of a dried-up monkey corpse attached to the back end of a fish. You probably weren't fooled, but in 1842, a lot of people were when P. T. Barnum exhibited a similar creation he called "The Feejee Mermaid."

Here are some seemingly impossible shapes you can make for yourself. All you need is some letter-sized paper, scissors, and tape.

 Try cutting one of your pieces of paper in two places, then folding it to look like this picture.

86 Cut a strip about one inch wide from the long side of the paper. Bring the ends together so they overlap a bit, then twist one end halfway around and tape the ends together. You've just made a Möbius strip. Run your finger along one side of the paper. Are there two sides or one?

87 If you cut the strip in half lengthwise, will you get two loops or one? Try it and see.

88 Cut the strip in half lengthwise again. What happens?

NOTE:
YOUR CUTS DON'T HAVE TO BE PERFECTLY STRAIGHT FOR THE ACTIVITY TO WORK.

GETTING OUT THE WORD

Sometimes words can be as misleading as pictures.

 Read the note below:

> If you think that I like you, you are
>
> sadly mistaken. Yes, you've read this
>
> right. I truly believe that you are
>
> stupid. That you can do anything right is
>
> simply amazing. Do me a favor and
>
> stay away from me. You will never
>
> be my friend. You know I mean it
>
> when I say I don't want to see you again
>
> because I always say what's in my heart.

Sounds pretty mean, doesn't it? Actually, it's a love note written in code. Can you figure it out?

90 There's an animal stretching over two or more words in each sentence below. How many can you find?

1. Jessica likes to do good deeds.
2. But, Bill, I only wanted to help.
3. When I grow up, I want to be a race car driver.
4. Sarah wants to be a very good student.
5. Let me sing or I'll act like a monkey.
6. Matt came looking for you yesterday.
7. Please put the frying pan there on the counter.

Can you read each of the following backward?

WOW   NOON   ROTOR   RACECAR

No lemons, no melon   Madam, I'm Adam.

Words, phrases, and sentences that read the same way forward and backward are called "palindromes." So are numbers. The year 2002 is a palindrome. Can you think up some of your own?

WHAT FOUR-LETTER WORD CAN BECOME ITS OPPOSITE IF YOU ADD ONE LETTER?

What do the words below have in common?

CODE   HIDE   DOCK

BIKE   KID   BOX

Give up? Turn the book upside down and hold it in front of a mirror. Can you still read the words? That's because the top half of each letter is the mirror image of the bottom half. This kind of word is called an "ambigram."

91 What's wrong with the sentence on the right?

A
bird
in the
the hand
is worth
two in the
the bush.

92 Write the letter "A" on a piece of paper. Now add one letter to make a new word. Keep adding one letter at a time to make another new word until you get from "A" to "ORANGES."

ORANGES

93 Tilt the page slightly down and away from you. Can you see the letters? What do they say?

BETTING THE NUMBERS

Numbers can be just as tricky as words and pictures.

 94 Look at the numbers on the right. Can you figure out the pattern and tell what the next number will be? Hint: Each number builds on the one before it.

> **1**
> **11**
> **21**
> **1211**
> **111221**
> **312211**
> **13112221**

95 Solve the problem on the right in your head by adding up the rows of numbers in groups.

> **1000**
> **20**
> **30**
> **1000**
> **1030**
> **1000**
> **20**
> _____

96 What number did these ancient Egyptian hieroglyphics stand for?

97 What four-letter word can you subtract three letters from yet still have five left and not change the word's meaning?

The figure below is called a "magic square." Why? Because no matter which direction you add the numbers up—as shown below, turned upside down, reflected in a mirror, or turned upside down *and* reflected in a mirror—the total will be 19,998.

1111	1888	8811	8188
8818	8181	1118	1881
1188	1811	8888	8111
8881	8118	1181	1818

COVERING UP

Dagmarr Rothman, the man on the cover of this book, could swallow a live mouse, wait a minute, then bring it back up again. Pretty disgusting, huh?

The movement on the cover is called a "lenticular effect." It was made from a few seconds of a film made in the 1940s. What you're seeing, though, is a bit of a trick. Because we could only use 22 frames to make the lenticular, the cover actually shows only the end of Rothman's act, when he's spitting the mouse out. When you move the book to see him swallow it, you're simply reversing the action just like you'd do with your VCR or DVD players. Here are the frames we used from the film.

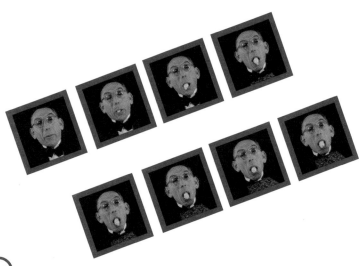

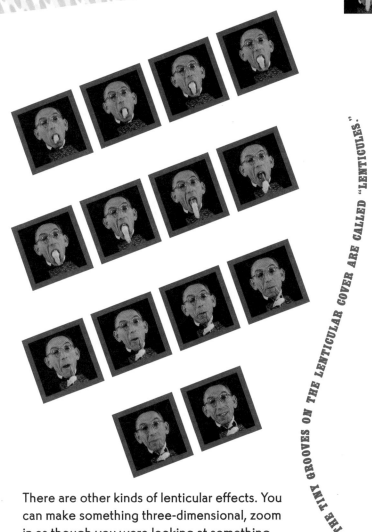

There are other kinds of lenticular effects. You can make something three-dimensional, zoom in as though you were looking at something through a microscope, or transform one object into another (this is called "morphing").

ANSWER KEY

1 You should see what looks like a hole in your free hand.

2 If you don't see the floating finger, try moving your hands a little closer or a little farther away. If that doesn't work, try changing the distance between your pointer fingers.

3 Your finger will look like it's jumping back and forth. If it only jumps with your left eye closed, your left eye is your "dominant" eye. If it only jumps with your right eye closed, your right eye is dominant.

4 You should be able to see three lines.

5 A second figure should appear.

6 The dog and cat should touch noses.

7 You should see "spokes" that appear to be moving inside the circle.

8 The two circles should appear to be moving in opposite directions.

9 There should appear to be flashing green dots where the lines intersect.

10 You may see colors as well as swirls.

11 Colors may appear to zigzag between the lines.

12 If you cannot see the number 5 in the bottom circle, you may have red-green color blindness.

13 The red diamonds are all the same shade.

14 The hazy spot will start to disappear.

15 The inner circles of the top pair are the same shade of yellow. The inner circles of the bottom pair are different shades of red.

16 All the green lines are the same shade.

17 You'll see the afterimage of a bright white lightbulb. The afterimage of the apple will appear red.

18 The afterimage of the lemon should look blue-green. The afterimage of the orange should look blue.

19 The white afterimage of the lightbulb should look brighter than the paper. When you look at a wall instead of paper, the afterimage appears to be larger. After you stare at an image for about 20 seconds, you should start to see a "halo" vibrating around the edges.

20 The lines should appear to be perpendicular to the page.

21 The fold at the "bottom" will look as though it's moving from side to side. When you look at the paper while standing up, it will also appear to be tilted backward.

22 Depending on how you see it, the cowboy and the horse may appear to be facing either way.

23 The upside-down face looks fairly normal because the eyes and mouth are right-side up. When you turn it upside down, it looks really weird for the very same reason.

24 The sides of the vase look like the profiles of two people facing each other.

25

26

27 The duck's beak turns into the rabbit's ears.

28 The young woman's face is turned away. Her jaw is the old woman's nose, her ear, the old woman's eye, and her necklace, the old woman's mouth.

29

30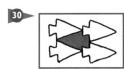

31 The shapes cut out of the squares make it appear that a triangle is overlapping them—but the triangle isn't really there.

32 This time there appears to be a square that isn't really there.

33 You can probably read the word "BELIEVE," but the letters aren't really there.

34 If you try to look directly at the pale circles, they disappear—or seem to move to another spot.

35 The picture shows concentric circles, not a spiral. This is easier to see when you cover half the picture with your hand. You can also try tracing the circles with your finger.

36 The shape is a square.

37 The circles are perfect.

38 The squares are perfect.

39 The figure on the left is a square. Dark colors look "heavier" than light colors, so the rectangle may look like it weighs more even though it's only a two-dimensional picture.

40 The lines of tiles are parallel.

41 The purple lines are straight.

42 None. All the lines are straight.

43 The lines may not look parallel, but they are.

44 The red bars are straight.

45 The center line is straight.

46 When you hold the picture close to your eyes, the checks should look as though they are straight.

47 The lines may look like they curve, but they are straight.

48 Both circles are the same size.

49 The area of the inner circle and the area of the outer ring are the same.

50 The arcs are all cut from circles that are the exact same size.

51 Whichever one is on the right will look bigger even though both are the same size.

52 The inner squares are both the same size.

53 The difference actually makes the three bands all look the same size.

54 The columns are all the same size. When white columns are set against a light background (like the sky), the columns appear thinner than when they are set against a dark background (like the inside of a building).

55 Both bars are the same size. This illusion was first drawn by Mario Ponzo in 1913 and is called the "Ponzo illusion."

56 The picture is flat, but because the bottom squares are drawn in perspective, they appear to be part of a floor meeting a wall.

57 The pictures of the boys are the same size, but if the boys were real, the one in the back would be taller because figures that are farther away look smaller than they really are.

58 The labeled lines in each set are the same length.

59 The brim is as wide as the hat is high.

60 Measured from the outer edges, the base is 630 feet wide.

61 The eyes are all the same distance apart.

62 The dot is midway between the top and bottom of the pyramid.

63 Yes, the green lines would form one line if they were connected.

64 The bottom green line.

65 The arcs would form a perfect circle.

66 No, the lines will meet in the middle to form perfect arches.

67 The pencil and your finger should look broken, just as the straw does.

68 When you put the cardboard or paper over the top of the glass, the stamp will seem to disappear.

69 The blind spot is very small, so your brain fills in whatever is missing.

70 If you look at the box long enough, it will seem to change direction.

71 You should be able to see the ladybug both inside and outside the box.

72 The basket should appear to switch direction.

73 You probably can't see them both at the same time.

74 You should be able to see both, but not at the same time.

75 If you see the bench from above, it looks sturdy. If you see it from below, it appears to be missing a leg.

76 You probably see the circles as a tube.

77 The different colors may make the circles look more distinct.

78 It may appear to be either up or down.

79 It may appear to curve either way.

80 Besides the diamond, there are squares and arrows.

81 This is called an impossible figure. It looks like it has three prongs on the bottom, but there are only two at the top.

82 This, too, is an impossible figure. You would not be able to build a triangle like this.

83 Shagena gave the bottle to Ripley only on condition that his secret would never be told! No one knows how he did it.

84 You could never reach the bottom of this never-ending stairway.

85

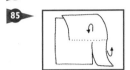

86 There is only one side.

87 You will get one loop.

88 You will get two loops.

89 To read the love note, start with the first line and read every other one.

90 1. dog; 2. lion; 3. bear; 4. beaver; 5. gorilla; 6. camel; 7. panther

91 Each "the" is repeated twice.

92 A, aN, Ran, ranG, rangE, Orange, orangeS

93 Robert Ripley

94

1	one, *which becomes . . .*
11	one one, *which becomes . . .*
21	two ones, *which becomes . . .*
1211	one two, one one, *which becomes . . .*
111221	one one, one two, two ones, *which becomes . . .*
312211	three ones, two twos, one one, *which becomes . . .*
13112221	one three, one one, two twos, two ones . . .

so the next number would be:

1113213211	one one, one three, two ones, three twos, one one

95 The answer is 4,100. Don't believe it? Try using a calculator.

96 1,235,326

97 Five. If you subtract *f, i,* and *e,* you still have *v,* the Roman numeral for 5.

Answers to Riddles:

Page 13: If a person with one eye looks at you, he or she will see your two eyes. But when you look back, you'll only see one eye.

Page 47: The carved figure grew bigger each year.

Page 55: The nail will be the same distance from the ground no matter how high the tree grows.

Page 69: If you add *t* to *here,* you'll get *there,* its opposite.